Secrets

Secrets

Memoir by
Hilda Stephens-Antoine

XULON PRESS

Xulon Press
2301 Lucien Way #415
Maitland, FL 32751
407.339.4217
www.xulonpress.com

© 2020 by Hilda Stephens-Antoine

All rights reserved solely by the author. The author guarantees all contents are original and do not infringe upon the legal rights of any other person or work. No part of this book may be reproduced in any form without the permission of the author. The views expressed in this book are not necessarily those of the publisher.

Unless otherwise indicated, Scripture quotations taken from the New King James Version (NKJV). Copyright © 1982 by Thomas Nelson, Inc. Used by permission. All rights reserved.

Printed in the United States of America.

ISBN-13: 978-1-63221-420-1

TABLE OF CONTENTS

Introduction: The Secrets We Keep vii

Greeting: My Memoir....................... ix

Chapter 1: My Journey 1

Chapter 2: New Adventure 7

Chapter 3: Memories to Grow By 15

Chapter 4: You Can Begin Again............23

Chapter 5: Digging a Little Deeper..........31

Chapter 6: Getting Closer 41

Chapter 7: Amazing Journey................51

Introduction

THE SECRETS WE KEEP

What is a secret? In my opinion, a secret is a hush-hush, don't tell, don't reveal any information regarding yourself or others!

In our society today, many people live with pain, hurt, and shame that haunt and terrify them for years, because they are afraid that someone will find out their best-keep secrets. In everyone's lives, there may be some things they are not proud to have done; yet they happened, and no one can find out just how they feel on that issue.

Secrets

I can truly say there are many things that happened in my life that I'm not proud of either, but when I became a born-again Christian, I knew within my heart that I could release my pains, my fears, and even my deep, dark secrets to God. I knew God would understand things about me that no one else would or could, so I decided to let go.

Greeting

MY MEMOIR

What you are about to read is my personal journey—things that started in my childhood and spilled over into my adulthood called *secrets*. I pray that after you read my memoir, you will discover that God is right here to deliver you from all the pains and hurts you may be carrying all alone.

Many of my secrets started before I knew Christ, some while I was learning about Christ, and others while living a life in Christ. If you have never made a mistake or experienced what most people have endured, then my memoir may not impress you, and that's okay; however, I'm sure you know someone who had a difficult life.

My memoir is not designed to air out dirty laundry or release confidential information, but to be a guide of spiritual healing, restoration, and renewal. I want to let you know we can be all that God has called us to be and more.

I'm here to encourage you in this moment; that you can take a deep breath and know you will get through all your secrets with God's help.

I'm releasing my memoir because the Spirit of God said it's time for the believers to get healed, strengthened, and given the life that God said we could live. I believe, if you open your heart to the truth, you will see what God has to offer to those of you who have been too afraid to let go of your secrets.

What I do know is that you will never regret spending time in the presence of God getting healed, renewed, and refreshed. You might not be challenged to write a book, but one thing's for sure: there is nothing better than standing before God knowing that you are healed, cleansed, saved, and filled with His spirit and love.

Chapter 1

MY JOURNEY

I remember that special day, the day that every girl dreams of—my wedding day. Yes, it was a very important day. But my wedding was not a happy one; it was the day I made the choice to do the right thing at the wrong time, with the wrong person. You see, it started long before that day. I needed someone to love me and only me.

I was brought up in a Christian home, but there were times in my family when there was loud arguing. Most of the time that came from my father,

Secrets

right after my mother had prepared one of her best meals. If anything ticked off my father, or he had a couple of drinks, boy, it was on and popping.

My father didn't have any trouble speaking what was on his mind. He was a caring and kind man who always prepared a way for his family.

I realized today that I have my father's best gift: speaking what is on my mind. You can bet no one has to second-guess where I'm coming from; yes, you always know.

That's not to say that I'm always right. I have learned how my words can affect others. But growing up before Christ entered my life, you can imagine I was too hot to handle.

There were nine siblings in my family, and there was always something to do and somewhere to go. We are a close-knit family because of prayers, love, and good times.

I was the sibling that did things my way. That's not to say my brothers and sisters didn't get into trouble—they were more cautious.

Growing up as a young girl, I pictured how my life would be. But today, I can say it's nowhere close to what I thought it would be. I made many mistakes along the way, but looking back over my life, I made some good choices too; but my secrets were just getting started.

Secrets can hurt a lot of people. That's why we avoid sharing the truth—because today they may be your family or friends, but tomorrow they might become your worst nightmares.

My secret began in my senior year of high school. I was so excited about graduation and going to college to major in fashion merchandising; I planned to own a boutique.

But what I feared the most was yet upon. I was pregnant! I thought my life was over, my world had ended, and I had let my family down. I would have been the first sibling to enroll in a major university.

Months passed. I did graduate but decided to work instead of going to college; bad decision for what was waiting down the road. People began

Secrets

asking questions: "Are you pregnant?" And my response: No way!

"Are you going to college?" *Yes, I am leaving soon.* I continued to the lie with a straight face and kept hiding what I knew was the truth from my sweet, dear mother. I knew this would kill her and break her heart.

I was so afraid and alone. I wanted to crawl in my mother's lap and confess my secret, to yell from the top of my lungs, "I messed up this time! My life is over! I have brought shame on my family!"

This was a different time than now. Today, everyone has a baby; you look out of place if you don't have one. But my advice: wait until God blesses you with the right mate to marry.

The only thing that helped me to survive my dilemma was the wonderful man that stood by my side. It's funny how things happen in your life and you don't know why. But I can tell you now—what you do in the dark will definitely come to light.

I was not ready for the light to shine on me, but it did, and now I had to deal with the truth.

My Journey

The last month of my pregnancy, my mother had enough. She kindly asked, "When is the baby due?" I looked at my mother, tears running down my face, and softly said, "Any day."

The only thing that gave me away was my fat, round face.

My secret was revealed. What joy it brought to my soul. I carried that secret all alone. I did learn from that lesson; I decided early in life, which was probably a mistake, never to have any more children.

I never married my daughter's father, but he was a great influence in our lives and supported her all the way. We finally decided we were just too young to get married and create more problems.

Life had more to offer, and after eight years, we went our separate ways. We always remained friends and parents to that special, little girl. I did get through that stressful time in the early years of my life, but there was much more in store for me.

Chapter Two

NEW ADVENTURE

I begin to search for what I should be doing with my life. I was a single mother with a young child. I decided to enroll in a program that was offered by Durham Technical College and sponsored at University of North Carolina at Chapel Hill.

I had a lot of support with my daughter; my mother was my built-in babysitter. I was headed for new adventures and couldn't wait to start the new program. I met many friends along the way,

Secrets

but only one true friend, Diane. We called her Lady Di before there was a Lady Di. If walls could talk, Diane should be writing this book.

We were gathered in class one morning, just having general conversations, when the ladies decided to take a break from studying.

Everyone began to talk about their personal lives. One by one, they went around the room sharing things: how many children they had, whether they were married or just in love.

It was my turn to share something about me. I could feel that pain of three years ago creeping back on me. One girl asked, "Do you have any children?"

"Children," I said. "I don't have time for a child; I'm trying to get my life together."

To my surprise, I was keeping a secret again; and I just knew no one would find out in my class, because I lived in the country and the other students lived in the city. My secret would be my secret again.

The next week, my daughter's father had made plans to keep his daughter; he decided to visit his

New Adventure

aunt. I didn't have any knowledge of this, but one of my classmates was her best friend. Remember what I said the week before about a child?

Monday morning, when the classroom was quiet, my classmates yelled out, "Hilda!" I quickly looked. "You got a beautiful daughter."

Everyone stared at me and asked, "When did this happen?"

I softly replied, "You got to be making a mistake."

"No way!" my classmate yelled again. "I met your daughter this weekend with her aunt, and there is no way you can deny that she is not your daughter."

My face was hot, and I was sweating all over the place. I could have socked her right in her big mouth.

Everyone in the class said, "That's nice, why are you ashamed?"

My answer: "I don't know." I got through that tough day with the help of my friend Diane. The next day, my friends and I drove to my mother's house to see that precious, little girl. I love my daughter so much. She was not the problem; I was.

Secrets

I still was not prepared for the lesson I thought I had learned. Life can be filled with struggles, trials, and fears. I couldn't escape the choices I made. My life became upside down, and I was walking in the dark. As the saying goes, there is always light at the end of the tunnel, but sometimes I wonder what tunnel.

I could talk myself in and out of everything. I realized I had played that tune before, and no one wanted to hear that song again. I continued my journey, keeping secrets, no matter how hard I tried to make things right.

My problems continued, and soon they became major problems. I wasn't ready for this one; I made a big mistake and it could have taken my life. My friends and I were out, having a great time, when suddenly this man appeared at our table. At first, I didn't recognize him, but it was the poor soul who had tried asking me out on a date for over a year.

We were friends, but I never asked the right questions. He asked me out that night, and finally I said yes; and boy, he was glad. We had a great time until we decided to go back to his place, and early in the morning is when it all happened.

This mysterious person entered the house, breaking the glass out of every window. My heart raced as I searched for a place to hide. I called out my friend's name, but he didn't respond. I had no idea what was going on and he was missing in action.

The woman appeared in the bedroom and fell across the bed. In my mind she was dead and I was going to be blamed for killing her, but by the grace of God I was able to escape the house, while vicious dogs chased me down the street. It was a night to remember.

I never looked back, and I didn't answer his calls. Eighteen years later, my friend apologized about that particular night; it was his ex-wife. No one got hurt, but my friend had carried this for so long. You can just guess; it was my secret.

Without God in your life, you will continue to struggle, be defeated, and lack in everything. I was still walking on the same path. My choices played a big role in my life and the lives of others.

Secrets

You've got to know when enough is enough. I stayed sad for years, from one relationship to another. I thought, if I could just find the right man, I would be so happy.

Baby, I needed to wake up and smell the coffee. I just missed the lesson. It's not about the man; it was all about me! I didn't know who I was or what made me happy. I found out that no one could make me happy because I didn't like myself. And that's the problem: We look to other people to make us happy.

I had many friends. I was the life of the party; I dressed very nicely, owned a car, and a rented an apartment I called home. Sometimes if things were good, I had some cold, hard cash. I knew I had it going on! But why was I so afraid to let anyone get close to finding out who I really was?

The purpose of my memoir is not to focus on what happened to me in life, but to share with you some of my most painful memories of keeping secrets.

New Adventure

I soon discovered that God was waiting to heal me from myself. I couldn't see the big picture; I didn't want to see the picture at all. This happens when you are so afraid to let go of all your fears and secrets.

God loves me so much, and He was waiting with His arms stretched wide opened, saying, "Come to Me and I will give you rest" (Matt. 11:28).

My transition wasn't easy, and I found myself not ready to let go, not just yet. That thing called a *relationship* has a way of breaking you down, especially if you are not in Christ.

Chapter Three

MEMORIES TO GROW BY

I had been saved for nine months, and I was saved by God's amazing grace. It was getting close to my special day. I decided not to have a big wedding—just a few friends and family.

Somehow, things changed a week before the wedding; to my surprise, I was not excited one bit. The sweet voice inside of me kept echoing, "You're making a mistake." I was just a babe in Christ, how was I supposed to know who was speaking to me?

Secrets

I guess you can imagine I went ahead with the wedding. Not with family or friends, just me and my man waiting for our number to be called at the justice of the peace.

No pre-marital counseling, no advice from anyone, because I didn't want anyone trying to talk me out of something that my man said he heard God say. What difference did it make? He was called by God. So, why would I be questioning God? Or, should I be questioning the man?

I was keeping secrets again. Why? Because we didn't tell a single soul. Let me clear something up: This was not the first marriage, that was a secret too. But it was over before it got started, so I never counted it.

Life was hard for me. I was trying to be a good wife, mother, and Christian all at the same time. These were tough jobs for me to balance. There were good and bad days, living in houses without electricity, or water, and sometimes without food. I learned to live with my circumstances, especially the abuse. I was married to a man who loved

God with a great ministry, who had a few secrets of his own.

My life continued to take a downward spin. I had some good days, but I had my share of bad days too. It took a toll on my mind, body, and spirit. I begin to think that God didn't care about me. How could He love me with all this pain?

The real problem was that the ups and downs would not allow me to admit my secrets, not even to God. I was done. Years came and quickly passed, as I tried to put my life back together. I worked so hard at everything and tried to keep everyone happy, especially my husband.

I arrived home early from work. My husband and I had a brief discussion about an issue. He didn't care for my response, and before I knew, he had punched me in the face and I was left to wear a nice, big, fat black eye.

I guessed my husband forgot he was scheduled to preach that night and that, of course, I had to go with him. When we arrived at the church, I tried to smile but I really couldn't see. Everyone stared at

Secrets

me, as I continued to make up stories about what happened to my eye.

There was no way I was going to let the cat out of the bag. I had to go home with this man. Secrets are not good things to keep; you can lose your life behind a secret if you don't ask for help or get help. *Secrets*, I thought to myself, *you are keeping secrets again, and this time your very life is at stake.*

I tried to leave my abusive relationship, but it was so hard. I was so consumed by what the people would say. This man was not an ordinary preacher; his very life was at stake. Someone always tried to kill him. He cast out demons, laid hands on the sick, and they recovered—yes, he walked in the anointing of God. I loved the man of God and the ministry, but I didn't love the man behind the mask.

It took fifteen years for me to finally say, "Enough is enough. I will not live in fear anymore because I serve an all-powerful, all-loving, all-knowing God." It wasn't that God didn't hear my cry or couldn't do anything about my problems. What was so disturbing was I never believed He could.

"God has come that we may have life and have it more abundantly, or to the fullness" (Jn. 10:10). I would not have an abundant life keeping secrets. God wanted me to be honest with Him. He already knew where I was. I had to come to grips with the fact that God's Word is true, no matter what I went through.

I finally decided that I was no longer responsible for the way people chose to live their lives, but I'm responsible for what I allow a person to do to me, especially if it is not in the will of God. I need to clarify this statement so you will know the content to the fullness.

If anything in your life is going against the will of God, please look at it. I could have stayed in that abusive relationship and continued to say, "God will work it out," and listened to some good, old church folks who said to stay; but I knew I had every reason to leave, because my husband was in denial that he had a problem.

Secrets

Although I had the facts and the proof, it was still hard to leave, until one day I decided to talk with someone about this problem.

One day after work, I met a close friend who gave me the most powerful advice anyone had given me. I poured my heart out; I just needed someone who was not close to my issue.

He listened intently and patiently until I could not say another word. He kindly leaned forward—not too deep, not too spiritual—and said these words that still resonate in my soul.

"The man of God, you love, but your husband is not worth a damn. The way he treats you, God is not pleased, and neither should you." Something inside of me leaped. I didn't know if this was the answer, but I was suddenly free, free, free in my mind, spirit, and soul. Something broke; it was enough for me. And until now, my friend always asks, "What did I do?" I can't explain it, but I will never be able to repay my friend for what he did for me.

He made me look Satan right in his ugly face and say, "You will not win this battle without a fight." The Word of God tells me, "To fight the good fight of faith" (1 Tim. 6:12). You might think I'm weak, but although you have told me I'm weak, I declare in Jesus's name that I can say, "Let the weak say I'm strong" (Joel 3:10). I will never again say I can't make it, because "With God all things are possible" (Matt. 19:26).

Chapter Four

YOU CAN BEGIN AGAIN

One by one, my secrets began to disappear; my life is in Christ. I finally believed that, "There was no more condemnation to those in Christ" (Rom. 8:1). After my divorce, I thought that my life was on track and I would never jump the tracks again. I found out that was not true at all.

The saints of old introduced me to this saying: Every new level brings about a new set of devils. And new it was. I began to pray to God about my life and what I should be doing now for Him. I

Secrets

started my quest looking for a new church home and new friends.

I went to many churches, but I didn't fit in. I have been in leadership and served as co-pastor for twenty years. What in the world could a girl do? I stayed in my apartment the entire weekend, depressed and alone. I wouldn't take a shower, comb my hair, brush my teeth, or clean the house. I wouldn't do anything.

After the divorce, everyone kept telling me how good I looked, but I wasn't feeling great. Do you not know looks can be deceiving? It took everything in my power not to drive my car off the bridge. There were times when I just wanted to die.

Depression is a killer; it has a way of sneaking up on you. I began to feel that pain all over again. I told myself I was keeping secrets and the whole world was finally going to find out. I was ashamed again. I was not able to tell myself the truth.

I started hiding my feelings again from my friends. I kept them guessing who I was. But it wasn't much different from the friends I had.

Everyone had a secret and it was hard to discuss it. We continued the same cycle repeatedly. So, I kept pretending everything was simply fine. I had an image to uphold, and there were things I shouldn't be doing. I was a preacher's wife, but I forgot that I was a Christian as well.

That changed; I had been saved for twenty years, so how did I find myself in a nightclub? This is my story. A long-time friend found out I had move back to Chapel Hill and things had been difficult for me, so she invited me out to a night on the town to have some fun.

When we arrived at the club, my heart was beating fast. I was so scared; God was going to get me, and this was not going to be good. I got myself together and went inside. The music was exactly right, and everyone was having fun; it was a relaxed atmosphere, just right for mingling and dancing.

I quickly took a seat, trying not to look so out of place. A fine gentleman walked over to the table and asked my friend to dance. She quickly said yes. I looked around the room nervously and saw this

Secrets

man walk toward my table. I quickly turned my head. He got the message and kept it moving.

I whispered under my breath, *Thank you, Lord*. But it was just the beginning. I couldn't escape the sound of that good music playing in my ear. By now, I was back to the good, old days—or that's what I thought.

I soon made a move to hit the dance floor, but I got the surprise of my life. The gentleman who asked me to dance was kind. He offered me a soda to drink, but there was something about him.

As we approached the floor for our dance, he started to stare at me, which made me extremely uncomfortable. I said to myself, *What's wrong with this brother?* He smiled, but I could tell he was troubled about something, and that something was me.

He leaned into me to ask me something, but by now, I was going into my church mode and trying to discern his spirit. Lo and behold, he was discerning mine. He whispered in my ear, "What are you doing in here?"

I was shocked. I smiled and said, "What do you mean?" And he repeated the question again, but this time with power, as he looked into my eyes. His eyes sent me a message. He said, "What are you doing in here? You don't belong in here."

My answer: "I paid my money just like you did to get in here."

But his response was, "Go home; this is not where you need to be. This is not you at all. Thank you for the dance." Then he walked me back to the table. My friend could tell I was upset about something, but she didn't ask any questions. I asked, "Can we please go now?"

As we exited the club, the gentleman saw me leaving and waved. All I could think of was, "If you make your bed in hell, I'm there" (Ps. 139:8). God had set me up with a guardian angel. You can call it what you like, but God got my attention.

After that experience, you would have thought I had it all together, but no, I didn't. If you stay around dust long enough, you will get some on you. That's exactly what happened to me; if you stay around sinners long enough, you will be sinning and sinning. I did big time. If you are going to tell the truth, well, why not tell the whole truth?

I was going from one extreme to another. I was going places I never been before, doing all ungodly and perverse things. It didn't matter to me; all I wanted was revenge. I didn't want to feel the pain, the hurt, the shame anymore. I discovered I was not healed completely.

I was still holding onto my past marriage and mistakes. I asked myself a thousand times, *What do you get when you try to live right and just be good to people?* My answer was not a smart one, and far from the truth. *All you get is kicked around and left out in the cold.* What I needed to do was to take a good look at what I was doing and why.

I felt betrayed by the man I loved and trusted with my life, my ex-husband. I was very much in love with someone who had moved on. Life was not good. I asked myself, *how could you be in this mess while walking with God for over twenty years?*

All my hurts, pains, and secrets had not been healed. Healing is a process—unless you allow God to heal you totally, you can find yourself in some places you thought you would never go. I had a secret, and I couldn't let this get out because I was preaching the Gospel of Jesus Christ and winning souls. How could I miss the mark? All I wanted God to do was allow the man I loved so much just to feel a little bit of my pain.

Chapter Five

DIGGING A LITTLE DEEPER

My purpose for writing this memoir is to let you know you can be healed and restored. God never gives up on us, and we should never give up on ourselves. I could never be all God intended me to be by keeping secrets.

But I continued the same path; I began to not have a conscience at all. I was drowning in my sorrow and getting further and further away from God. I couldn't remember if I was coming or going. I would ask myself, *who are you?*

Secrets

I could no longer hear God's voice or feel His power working through me. I would pray, but the answer never seemed to come. I missed the time we spent together, and how the Spirit would always guide and direct me. I asked God to forgive me of my sins, and that lasted for six months.

I struggled, and I would eventually end back up in the same patterns. The man, the ministry, and the marriage were gone. I still missed everything after twenty years. The funny part? I had dealt with someone that loved God just as much as I did, but he had a few secrets of his own.

My secrets weren't funny anymore; I couldn't continue to hold the man hostage of the things that happened in my life. My body and mind were so tired. The Lord has a way of just letting you go. In all my confusion, God turned my life around. I realized I was in God's hands; this was the turning point in my life.

Once again, life was good. It's always good when you have God in your life. I made some good choices, but sometimes the madness doesn't stop.

Life was getting better, but it wasn't easy. I had to pray, fast, and spend time with God. I needed everything I was doing and then more.

Don't let anyone fool you: only what you do for Christ will last. Staying on my course with God, I decided to ask for one of my most precious desires. Could I ever love again? My love increased the more for God, but not for a man. I was out to get everything.

My mind quickly shifted; I couldn't continue to keep secrets. I knew this wouldn't work because I was not that kind of person—and besides, God wouldn't allow me to get away with misusing His people.

No matter how I looked at life, life was always looking back at me.

Time passed quickly and I became exhausted in my prayers to God. My head was filled with all types of questions: God, do You really care about me? Why haven't You answered my prayers? God, are You upset with me? Why have You left me all alone? This sounds so sad, but it was true.

Secrets

God always knows more than we do, and His eyes are always upon us. I continue to search and search for answers. I finally came to grips with myself: I was keeping secrets again, but not from God. I was still troubled about my past. It's good to rediscover some things about yourself and how you can make some changes for your life. I was mad with God for not punishing the man that had brought so much pain to my life.

Why didn't God do something to make him pay for all the bad things he did to me? He made my life a living hell. Well, if you ask God anything, He always has an answer, even if you don't like His response. I didn't speak these thoughts out verbally, but they were in my heart.

God never answers our prayers the way we think He should, but He does answer our prayers. Sometimes we just don't recognize it. God is full of compassion and He knows what's best for us. We can rely upon His faithfulness. Weeks went by and there were little changes in my life.

I continued in faith because God cannot lie. I asked my questions, and my head became pretty filled when it came to the matters of the heart. I realized that I asked God for something that was in His will, and He was ready to bring the answer to me, but was I ready to deal with a man right now? Could I handle the commitment and the work required? Had I given myself enough time to find out who I truly was? I didn't want to repeat the same, old story.

I begin to break away from my fears and search with my heart and spirit. Yes, the answer finally came, and I was not happy with the outcome. I was not ready to deal with this thing called LOVE.

I continued to search, but this time my life took another turn. I drowned myself in my work and ministry. I kept busy. I wouldn't have time to find true love, and true love couldn't find me.

By now, this was all I had time for:

- Time to think
- Time to pray

Secrets

- Time to read
- Time to work
- Time to sleep
- Time to eat

And time to eat and eat some more. I couldn't work enough; I couldn't read enough; I couldn't pray enough. I was all prayed out. So, where do you go from here? I decided the best thing to do was "Be Still." And still I was, day after day, month after month. Nothing in sight! What did I want God to do?

I wanted God to teach me how to love again. I needed God's help in this matter. I couldn't get through this any other way.

I could not live with my own thoughts on this subject. Only God could teach me what real love was all about. Not the physical love, nor the love that you show toward your parents or another person, but the agape love.

God showed me He could make a difference in my life. I had to put my trust in Him. I never had to second-guess God. He prepared my spirit, and I became free and strong. I relied upon His strength to get me through the day. My secrets were disappearing. My mind, soul, and spirit felt so alive.

I guess you are wondering what is next, and so did I. The pain in my heart seemed to never stop aching. I began to believe that this was the way it was going to be. Could I really change what happened? Could I get somebody or anybody to believe in me again? I had to look at the problem for what it was worth and deal with it.

Running away has never solved anything. Hoping it will go away won't work either.

I felt so ashamed of the choices I made. God is our only support in a bad situation. "He will never leave you nor forsake you" (Heb. 13:5). God was right by my side in my most difficult moments. My secrets slowly disappeared, but I realized that my life was not over. A good Scripture to remember is Luke 8:17:

Secrets

For nothing is secret that will not be revealed, nor anything hidden that will not be known and come to light.

God's Word is true, and we cannot expect to get away with anything. He wants us to live in peace and harmony, not in fear.

God has not given us the spirit of fear, but power and love and of a sound mind(2 Timothy 1:7).

When we hide our secrets, we live in fear of someone finding out our past, our mistakes, and our pains. This is not the plan that God had for my life, and neither is it the plan for you.

The more I let go of my secrets, the more I enjoyed the benefits of God's blessings flowing in my life.

I had many ups and downs, twists, and turns, but I continued to pursue after God. It came to a point where I thought I was running out of time. But this was the time to embrace life and reach my full potential. My spirit reached the place where I belonged, and that was in the presence of God.

Digging a Little Deeper

I realized I couldn't figure out the plan of God for my life on my own, so I let go and decided just to trust Him and move on. It's funny how a secret puts a hold on your mind and leaves you to believe your life is over. Letting go isn't easy, but you can do it.

The remarkable thing about secrets: I could have let them go, but the fear and the mistrust kept me bound. The good news is I began to talk about my secrets, and that helped me gain a new life and new strength. God provided me with everything I needed to live a whole and complete life with joy.

Chapter Six

GETTING CLOSER

Secrets are a part of everyone's lives, but it all depends on how you deal with them. My secrets kept me a prisoner within my own gates. Everything I was looking for was inside of me, staring me right in my face.

My time spent with God is a rewarding and teachable experience. My love for Christ is all that I have. I'm convinced that I will survive every heartache and disappointment that life tries to offer me.

Secrets

Secrets must be confessed to God in prayer. All I had to do was ask God for forgiveness, and He brought restoration back to my life. God wanted to be first in my life, and all I had to do was give Him the glory.

If we confess our sins, He is faithful and just to forgive us our sins and cleanse us from all unrighteousness (1 John 1:9).

The problem is solved, and the case is closed. God knows more about me than I know about myself. The more I thought about writing my memoir, the more I could feel the joy deep in my heart that I was doing the right thing.

I did not need to be afraid any more about what people thought of me. I am who I am! First a born-again believer, who loves the Lord with all my heart and soul; a woman with class, style, and value; a friend with a listening ear and a caring heart; a mother and grandmother. And yet in all of this, it did not change that I kept secrets.

So, on the behalf of all my sisters and brothers, let the words on these pages give you the encouragement you need to set yourself free, free, free from yourself. I won't try to convince you that you won't have any pains, fears, worries, trouble, or even some repercussions about letting your secrets go. Just know that if you go to God, you just made the first step (and maybe the last step) you need to take.

Let God lead you in the way you should go—nothing is more important than this. You might be wondering why I'm doing this now. But if you are still carrying the pains of yesterday, or the thought is still fresh in your mind, I recommend it's time to let it go.

I had an awfully hard time. Remember, I was in an abusive relationship, so sharing my testimony about my marriage wasn't easy, but I can recall one Sunday morning in church in 1998. All I planned to do was give God praise, but something remarkably happened.

I stood to my feet and opened my mouth and told the story. People were in disbelief, some cried, and others were plain shocked. I couldn't stop; I

Secrets

didn't want to stop. That secret had been stuck to me for twenty years. It was like an eruption from a volcano; it kept flowing and flowing.

When my testimony ended, people were shouting, praising, dancing, and rejoicing with me. God had set me free, and so many others had received the deliverance of a lifetime.

Revelation 12:11 gives us a great example of what happened: "And they overcame him by the blood of the Lamb and the word of their testimony."

The church was filled with joy, and the saints received God's best because my testimony was filled with love and forgiveness.

My secret was out! I finally confessed that even after my divorce, I was still living a lie. I was not faithful to anyone, especially to God, who was there with me all the time. My outlook on life had a totally different perspective. That Sunday, God got all the glory.

I'm working on the next step. If I have any sisters or brothers who are afraid of being alone, let me hear you say "Amen." Being alone is a secret we are just ashamed of. There were times when I didn't want to go home. I would call everybody, asking the same questions.

"What are you doing? Are you busy? Would you like to go out?" I know it might sound familiar. It's a secret and no one can know. It might sound strange, but oh yes, it's real, and many have to deal with it.

Hey, I know you have been thinking. If you are single and have reached the age of thirty still alone, you may be wondering, *where is my mate to fill the void in my life?* Here is the kicker: first of all, most of us are not real about this matter. We try to find other things to fill that void in our lives.

We go to church, Bible study, sing on the praise team, and have important roles in the church, but we are too ashamed to let anyone know we want someone in our lives. I have seen this game too many times. How do I know? I played the game many times.

If I could figure out how to get through this, I would have my own TV show. We must face the problem head-on and become honest with ourselves.

We need the Father's help. He will lead and guide us in all things, even in the decision of what mate is supposed to be in our lives. When we get too anxious, we set ourselves up for trouble, which may lead to a path of destruction. Sound familiar? I know I'm right about this topic. It's a sensitive subject and the church doesn't want to talk about it.

In this day and time, anything goes, but a Christian cannot go with the flow. Christians are at an all-time high for divorces, teenage pregnancies, abusive relationships, and sexual misconduct, and they are secrets within the church.

Christians no longer feel they can consult with their pastors for godly advice. The church has almost become a social gathering where believers no longer trust God for guidance but continue in their own way. God expects us to seek after Him with all our hearts, minds, and souls.

"If I regard iniquity in my heart, the Lord will not hear" (Ps. 66:18). God will answer our prayers if, "We create a clean heart and renew a right spirit within us" (Ps. 51:10).

So, our secrets continue; it's a cycle that's hard to break. I know by now if you don't stand for something, you will fall for everything.

Here is my personal story on love, my greatest secret of all time. After years of being abused, I felt like I could never trust a man again, even if he said he was a born-again Christian. The wait to find Mr. Right can sometimes turn out to be Mr. Wrong. Many women have a hard time with this. We expect someone great for our lives, but sometimes, we end up with the short end of the stick. We look for love in all the wrong places.

When you allow the wrong person in your life, you can just imagine the pain and the heartaches that will come your way. The secret of this madness is the person you have invited into your life and the behavior you have allowed to take place.

Watch for the signs; they are always there if you just take time to look. No one is perfect, but if you have left God out of the equation, not waiting for

Secrets

His guidance is a big mistake. Matters of the heart can get the best of believers. You might be thinking, *this won't happen to me*, but I can guarantee, just keep living. It will show up somewhere.

Never let your faith in God become second and your new partner become first. If he or she can't get with the program, then it's time to change the channel. It was a different time in my life. I was all alone, not sure who I could trust. Just when I thought I had it all together, I lost my brother and sister fighting the battle with cancer.

My family depended upon me for strength and support after the death of my siblings. I was worn out and too tired to quit. I needed someone I could lean on for just a short while but didn't want anyone to think "Miss Superhero" needed anyone to help her out.

However, I was a mess. I held it together for so long. I screamed, "God, help me get this right!" Now that I have someone special in my life, what do I do with all these emotions of fear and anxiety?

Getting Closer

I could feel my face getting hot and hands sweating, my inside screaming, "It's happening again. You got a secret, and everyone is going to find you out." Well, I did have a secret: I was in love. I think.

My new relationship caused my faith to be on trial, and I was tested by leaps and bounds. My life was turned upside down. Could I stand the test and the pressure? Living for God and trying to please people—and, let me keep it real, trying to please my man—made me rethink my obligations.

You don't have to sell out if you mess up; ask God for forgiveness. I surely did mess up. My secret was out again, but during all these trying times and tests, I became a better Christian; one who learned not to be so quick to judge other Christians.

We all want to live lives that please the Lord, but sometimes we fall short of His glory. Like King David, I wanted to be a woman after God's heart. So, I decided to live a life that pleased God, even if it meant that I would be alone.

Secrets

My personal story is that I did mess up as a Christian, but I didn't stay there. I had to learn how to deal with my consequences. Having sex with a man or woman will not get you what you thought but will only leave you feeling deprived and having a broken fellowship with God.

Trying to change a person's mind that's already made up will not help you get what you want. Stand your ground and wait for the best that God has to offer you. It will be better than you can imagine.

Chapter Seven

AMAZING JOURNEY

The greatest fear the devil wanted me to encounter was that I keep this hidden from some of the greatest people I taught to trust God with all their hearts. I now know why God wanted me to write this memoir in this season of my life. You can read between the lines.

Living a life for Christ is a rewarding blessing, and things can sometimes get bent out of shape; but God keep blessing me, because I learned to tell the whole truth.

Secrets

God has given me one of the best congregations in the world: just ordinary people looking for someone to be an example, tell the truth, keep it real, and truly allow themselves to be transparent. Now they will understand why they can't get over on God and their pastor. It's called a life trusting and experiencing God.

My love for Christ made all the difference in my life. Although I made some bad choices and many mistakes, my life now is so rewarding. The things I discovered along the way have given me the fortitude to stand when there is nothing else to do but keep standing.

I want the world to know we have a Savior who died for all our sins. Even when you fall, you can get back up again. I learned from my mistakes. I confessed my sins to God, and I repented, which means to turn away from.

The point I want to get across is that God has given me this opportunity to witness to the body of Christ and say that we all can be free, breathe, and live life to its fullest potential. My memoir is written with a whole lot of people in mind who may be too afraid to get healed and set free. Here is your opportunity to release yourself from the pain and shame of your past.

It's over now, and there is nothing I have to be ashamed about anymore. You might be thinking that's no secret, but they were secrets to me, and they played big parts in my life. If you are reading my memoir, don't be so quick to judge me or people like me.

I got my secrets out of my system now—and besides, before I get too famous, there will be nothing anyone else can tell. My journey has kept me learning in my most trying times to believe God, no matter what is happening or shaking around me. I have learned that God is all you've got all the time. He may seem far, far away, but He is closer than you think.

As Christians, we should strive to live lives that please the Lord. I want you to understand we shouldn't be so ready to point the finger, trying to

Secrets

tear down our brothers and sisters when they fall short of the glory of God.

I'm not saying that we should continue to walk in disobedience, either. Remember, God hates sin! When we sin, we must be ready to deal with the outcome. God loves us and He desires the best for us.

He is ready to bless those who continue to walk upright and listen to His command. I believe if the church would teach the principles of forgiveness and repentance, the body of Christ would be stronger, healthier, and more mature saints.

The body of Christ sometimes feel like no one understands their problems, situations, and concerns. We can make saints feel that they will be ridiculed for falling short because they are Christians, but we all fall short and, maybe you forgot, there was someone there to help you get back up.

There is no special formula, waving of the hand, or owner's manual: it's just a matter of trusting God. God has shown His compassion to His children a thousand times over. He will never leave or forsake us. He is there to the end of time.

I have discovered that, "If God be for me, none can be against me" (Rom. 8:31). I reach new heights every day. I can look in the mirror and say I know I belong to the King of Kings; and if you have any questions about me, just ask my Father, who now is well pleased.

I'm so excited every day, because I know God is at work for just little, old me. My faith in God made me a true believer that God's Word works, and I can take that to the bank.

God can do the impossible if you are willing to wait for the impossible move of God in your life. All you must do today is learn the lesson; it's quite simple. Learn to trust God in all that you do, so only what you do for Christ will last.

This is your time to set the record straight; I know you are still hiding! Go ahead, let it go! God's way is the best way. When problems and circumstances begin to look dark in my life and my faith is unsettled, I immediately find some Scriptures that promise me the answer and reach back and get my testimony that pulls me through.

Secrets

I quickly remember that what He did back then, He certainly can do again. It wasn't easy sharing my story, but here is some good news: When this memoir was first birthed in me, and I started the rough draft in 2000 and put it aside, I knew I would have to revisit it one day. I closed with these words: "I haven't got the ring and I still haven't walked down the aisle, but I have so much more."

Time passed. I continued my journey with God, and amazing things began to happen. I found the key to life. It was staring at me right in my face and heard this word: preparation. Get ready! And ready I did.

I began to dream big; it all started for me. For five years, I went on a supernatural, I-believe-I-can-have-what-I-say confession. My soul was ready!

I cleaned, painted, and redecorated my house. I got new carpet, new hard wood floors, new furniture, new sinks, etc. I did a complete overhaul.

Next, I went to my closets and removed everything. I gave away shoes, dresses, suits, handbags, jewelry, and makeup. I was ready for whatever God had for me. I really didn't understand what was happening, but I kept it moving.

When the Spirit spoke, I moved. I begin to confess before others that I was preparing for my husband. There was not a single man in sight, but that didn't stop me. I didn't ask God any questions.

I got my instructions from God, and He told me to be prepared. Two years went by, but that didn't stop me from confessing what I knew to be true. Ladies, I kept it moving, teaching, and preaching like a wild woman.

This confession had become so real in my spirit. I knew my husband was close by. I didn't try to figure out anything; I didn't go looking anywhere.

Another year passed, but my faith wasn't shaken. Not one date, not one phone call, and still no man in sight. I didn't get discouraged at all, and soon other people begin to believe what I was confessing to be true.

My church members began to say, "I had a dream about you last night." Everyone was talk about a wedding.

Secrets

Finally, I met someone, and I knew he was exactly right for me and that he was the one. I hate to say it was a brief relationship—he was a perfect gentleman, a God-fearing man who loved his family. I must say I was heartbroken, but my plea to God was nothing like I expected.

In my quiet time alone with God, I looked up and said, with a grateful heart, if this man was in my life for just a brief moment just to show me what a God-fearing man looks like, so be it. I shouted, "God, I give You glory!"

It was the best answer that I could have ever said with my heart filled with joy; nothing more and nothing less. It was my turn-around season for me: meeting Mr. God-sent Man. Almost another year had passed, but this time, something happened.

My girlfriend, Betty, called me from Florida with a story about an amazing man she had met. This was in spring of 2016. After she talked over the information with her husband, he didn't think it was a good idea. He was only trying to protect me—he called me his little sister.

I didn't get mad. I only replied that God had me, and I continued my journey. Something inside of Betty wouldn't let her rest, however. Nine months later, after Christmas, Betty called again. Her first words to me were, "He's here."

"Who's there?" I asked.

Betty answered, "Please talk to him."

"I'm not doing this," I said. "God's got me."

Betty pleaded with me, "I'm going to give him the phone." The funny thing, her husband didn't say one word, so Betty knew what her assignment was. I finally agreed.

The man quickly said, "Hello," with an accent, and I said, "Hello," back. We talked for fifteen minutes. Betty quickly returned back to the phone and asked, "What do you think?"

I answered, "I'm not doing this!"

Betty wouldn't stop. "Hilda, can I give him your number?"

I shouted "No" three times, but Betty wouldn't let up. I gave in and said, "You can give him my number, because I definitely don't want his."

Secrets

A week later, I got the call that changed my life forever. For eleven months, we embraced a spiritual connection and we finally met in November 2017. God was the center of everything we did.

What I learned the most was that I didn't have to do anything. I made the decision early in the courtship: God, if this is the right man, he will pursue me, and I will be still and know that you are God (Ps. 46:10). I only called when he asked me to return his call.

It didn't matter if he didn't call or I missed our conversations. I wouldn't get in the way of God's plan. I wouldn't give myself a reason to call. Ladies, you know how we do. God worked on his heart, and He worked on keeping my mind straight.

After one year and five months, my Mr. God-sent Man popped the big question before twenty-five of my family members, and our big wedding day happened on December 31, 2018 after a two-year courtship. I want you to know everything was planned and God didn't leave anything out. God brought three states together—Betty from Florida, my husband from Georgia, and myself from North Carolina. So, to all of you out there that think God is not listening to your prayers, you better think again.

As I come to the end of my spiritual journey, I must thank my wonderful family who has always been there for me. My church family, Uplift Outreach Ministries, who gives me the utmost respect and love; to my friend Diane for over forty years of friendship; to my friend Dr. Annabelle, who always prayed me through many times; and to Betty, who God used and who wouldn't stop believing that this was my God-sent man. And yes, to my only daughter, Tesha, who is just over the top because Mom finally got someone in her life that she adores too.

So, as I come to the close of my memoir, it has been truly a blessing. Whatever is still trying to hold you back, "Let it go!" God has a wonderful blessing just waiting for you. And now I can finally say it with pure joy and peace:

Secrets

I got my ring and I walked down that aisle, and I was a beautiful bride. I almost forgot the groom was looking good too. I love you all.

Be blessed,
Your Sister in Christ
Ann Stephens Antoine, Apostle

Lightning Source UK Ltd.
Milton Keynes UK
UKHW021827141120
373340UK00010B/225

What is a Secret? Something concealed from others!

What you are about to read is my personal memoir on how God delivered me from fears, pains, past hurts, and abusive relationship. I pray that after you read about my personal journey, you will discover that God is right by your side to free you from all your pains, fears, and deep secrets you have carried too long.

My secrets started before I knew Christ, while learning about Christ and living a life in Christ. I am releasing my memoir because the Spirit of God said it is time to help believers get healed, strengthened, and live the life God promised.

My memoir is not about airing out dirty laundry or releasing confidential information, but a guide of spiritual healing, restoration, and renewed mind. My journey has not been easy; there were times I did not know what path to take even when I thought God was leading me. So how did I, a woman who loves God, who teaches and preaches God's Word, find herself in a night club?

Being born as a gifted storyteller not only helps Hilda bring the Word of God alive to each listener's ear, their hearts are changing and captivated through the Holy Spirit. Hilda Stephens-Antoine is the Founder and Pastor of Uplift Outreach Ministries and for 36 years, has been a mentor, motivator, and Women's Fellowship Conference speaker.

Hilda is a prolific lyricist of thirty-five song lyrics, writer and actress of three stage plays that were performed at the Art Center and Uplift in Orange County in North Carolina; and published author of the Book Series, "God Is This My Man." Hilda and her husband, Anthony, live in Durham, North Carolina. Hilda has one daughter, son-in-law and three grandchildren.